AUTUMN WISDOM

Finding Meaning in Life's Later Years

TEXT AND PHOTOGRAPHY
BY JAMES E. MILLER

Augsburg
MINNEAPOLIS

To my parents, Dorothy and Herman,
living examples of autumn wisdom.

ACKNOWLEDGMENTS

There is a deep sense in which this book is not "of me"—it is merely "through me." Many of my elders, both living and dead, are the authors of these thoughts. Two voices are particularly prominent: Ruth Lane and Myrl Aldrich. The enduring spirit of Helen Wade is contained here. Carol Tice offered ideas for the "suggestions" pages. Bob Klausmeier edited everything—text, quotations, and photography—with his unfailing penchant for simplicity and taste. Throughout it all, Clare Barton was more than my co-worker—she was my ballast. And always, always Bernie was there, and for that I am more than grateful—I am humbled.

AUTUMN WISDOM
Finding Meaning in Life's Later Years

The paper used in this publication meets the minimum requirements of American National Standard for Information Sciences—Permanence of Paper for Printed Library Materials, ANSI Z329.48-1984.   ∞

Manufactured in the U.S.A.   AF 9-2834

99   98   97   96   95   1   2   3   4   5   6   7   8   9   10

Library of Congress Cataloging-in-Publication Data and other copyright information will be found at the end of this book.

FOREWORD

We are growing older—and we're not alone.

By the year 2030, one in three Americans will be 50 or older. Yet despite increasing numbers of older people, our culture is slow in coming to terms with aging. Inaccurate stereotypes of older age still linger. Misconceptions about diminished physical and mental capabilities abound. Ageism, like racism and sexism, continues to limit large groups of people and to restrict individual lives. For these and other reasons, it can be painful to grow old.

This book is one tiny effort to reverse things. The thoughts presented here grew out of my experiences with people much older than I. In my late twenties I began developing a ministry with older adults in the first congregation I served as a clergyman. As I grew closer to dozens—and later hundreds—of older people, I was caught off guard by the amazing vitality I discovered. I found levels of understanding and compassion and acceptance that never failed to inspire me. I encountered examples of courage and resilience and fortitude that far surpassed anything I'd seen in my generation. My respect for my elders kept doubling, year after year.

Autumn Wisdom represents the lives of those many energizing, growing, inspiring persons who shared their hopes, beliefs, and wisdom with me. Now that I am poised between middle- and older-age myself, I am keenly aware that what these people taught me is worth preserving—for myself, for others, and hopefully, also for you.

Jim Miller

Fort Wayne, Indiana

Autumn arrives so quickly.
Even if you think you're ready for it,
you're never quite ready.
It comes so easily, so naturally.
Once there were signs of growth all around.
Then the colors begin to shift
and life begins to pull in upon itself.

In autumn you come to realize
    that the time you have before you
        is less than the time behind.
The possibilities you can entertain have narrowed.
There is a tension in the air.
You feel so young,
    yet you know you're growing older.
You feel so sure, and so uncertain;
    so experienced, and so uninformed.
You have learned so much,
    and there is so much yet for you to discover.

You have, in the autumn of your life, a rare opportunity.
From this perspective—one you've never had before—
    you can view your life from a distance.
You can see where your years have led you,
    what they have given you,
        what they have taken from you,
            how they have formed you.
You can also look into your future and plan and hope and dream.
And you can take the time to look for something
    you've always been looking for,
        even if you haven't put it into words:
            the meaning in your life.

Like many others you may have wondered,

Who am I, really?

What is my purpose on earth?

What have I learned and what am I meant to learn?

How am I to spend what precious time I have left?

The questions you ask and the answers you seek are spiritual ones.

They do not flow easily into words,

for they come wrapped in mystery.

But you dare not let that stop you from asking your questions

and from seeking your answers.

For in a very real sense, your entire life depends upon it.

This season of your life is a wonderful time to look for meaning.
It's a perfect time to think about your being born and your living
and your aging and your dying,
and what it all means from a spiritual point of view.
Now is a marvelous time to take the path
that carries you through sacred terrain,
where you can be reminded of all that waits for you.
There is no better place and there is no better time
than right here,
right now.

Your journey through life is uniquely yours.

You are your own person.
You have lived your own original life,
   and you will die your own unique death.
You dare not expect, therefore,
   that your journey will be everyone's journey.
Come autumn, some people are serene and some are passionate.
Some are hopeful, and others are afraid.
Some are hesitant, and others are bold.
You are called to make your own personal quest.
Like every seeker who ever lived,
   like everyone who ever *will* live,
      you must walk your own walk,
         and you must discover for yourself.

Your task is to seek what is timeless and true.
And the place to begin is right where you are.
The place to look is deep within yourself.
Following your chosen path requires courage.
For you can never be sure what you will find,
    or when you will find it, and where, or how.
Unless you begin your search,
    and unless you persevere,
        the answers you seek will not be *your* answers.
They will belong to someone else.
In the autumn of your life, you stand to miss too much
    to allow that to happen.
So find the path that you believe leads to meaning.
And then follow it.

Thus says the Lord:
"Stand by the roads, and look,
and ask for the ancient paths,
where the good way is;
and walk in it,
and find rest for your souls."

JEREMIAH 6:16

Those who would see wonderful things
must often be ready to travel alone.

HENRY VAN DYKE

Does the road wind uphill all the way?
Yes, to the very end.
And does the journey take the whole long day?
From dawn to dusk, my friend.

CHRISTINA ROSSETTI

- Take time to explore how you feel about entering the autumn years of life. What words best describe your feelings: contented? eager? hopeful? regretful? fearful? determined? Chances are, your feelings are mixed. You may want to keep a journal to track and understand this time in your life. An excellent way to begin the journal is by recording the emotions you've just explored.

- Study a photo of yourself from your early adult years. Ask: "In what ways was I the same then as I am today? In what ways am I now different?" Make a list of the similarities and differences you're especially proud of.

- Picture the journey your life has already taken. Map it out chronologically on paper, listing places that have been important to you: cities, states, countries you've lived in; addresses of your homes; names of schools, congregations, places of work. Add important events that influenced you in these places. As you study this "map" of your life, think about the strange twists and turns your journey has taken. Pause to consider how and why you moved from place to place in your life.

- Now think about how you'd like that journey to continue. Where would you like to be in the years ahead? Are there places you'd like to visit? What would you like to do and see? Who are some people you'd like to spend time with? Add these wishes, names, and places to another page of your map. Consider what you will do.

Your time of decline is a time of ascent.

A peak has been passed.

A turn has been made.

Nature is having its way, as nature always does.

But the way of nature is not the way of the spirit.

They operate on different principles,

    they follow different laws,

        and that's easily forgotten.

Yes, physically you decline; outwardly you begin to diminish.

But inwardly and spiritually, the opposite happens.

The spiritual part of you *grows* with age.

It becomes richer, fuller.

It has *more* to offer, not less.

It has something greater to share with the passing years.

It climbs higher.

O r, more accurately, the spiritual part of you *can* climb higher. But it will do so only if you allow it:

> only if you make time in your life to reflect;
>
> only if you give yourself the opportunity
>> to see what has long been waiting for you;
>
> only if you allow yourself the chance
>> to listen to what you've always been meant to hear.

A twelfth-century prayer expresses this autumn hope:

> *O Lord,*
>
> *May the end of my life be the best of it.*
>
> *And may my closing acts be my best acts.*

In the autumn of your life you can come to realize

> that what this prayer asks for is within your grasp—
>> your closing acts *can* be your best acts.

All you have to do is follow your spirit,

> and follow *the* Spirit.

It is a mistake to regard age
as a downhill grade toward dissolution.
The reverse is true.
As one grows older one climbs with surprising strides.

GEORGE SAND

O Thou full of compassion,
I commit and commend myself unto Thee,
in whom I am, and live, and know.
Be Thou the Goal of my pilgrimage, and my Rest by the way.
Let my soul take refuge from the crowding turmoil of
worldly thoughts beneath the shadow of Thy wings;
let my heart, this sea of restless waves,
find peace in Thee, O God.

SAINT AUGUSTINE

- Think about the spiritual part of yourself. How is it most comfortable expressing itself? Alone, or with others, or both? Silently, or with words, or with music? By doing something, or by doing nothing? Do you give your spirit enough expression? If not, how can you provide more time for this important endeavor? Plan to make time for your spirit at least once each day.

- Create a brief personal history of your spiritual life. Start by listing your earliest spiritual feelings. What were your childhood ideas about God and prayer? What was your image of God when you were twenty? How do you picture God now? What questions about God and faith do you still want answers to? How much of your prayer time is spent seeking and listening for God's voice? Turn this history into a faith journal that explores your questions. Set aside time to make daily entries. Use the book to reflect on your faith and your understandings of God.

- Go back to the twelfth-century prayer about your closing acts being your best acts. Meditate quietly on those words. Prayerfully consider what your "best acts" might be. Then make the prayer a daily part of your spiritual life.

- Begin each morning by bringing to mind two new things you have to be thankful for. These can be either little or large things. Recall these two things from time to time throughout your day.

In the fading light, you can see more clearly than ever.

Nighttime comes sooner in autumn.

Eyesight grows dimmer.

But when you expect to see less,

  it's possible to see more.

You can look back across the years

  and see patterns you would not see from a closer perspective.

You can view your life more completely.

You can grasp all that has happened to you with greater acceptance.

You can know the privilege of having experienced more,

  gathered more,

    filtered more.

And what you have filtered can help you,

  both as you look back and as you peer ahead.

There is something else you see better than ever, and that is yourself.
When you look inward, you use a different kind of eyesight,
  one that becomes more keen with the years.
You become more clearly yourself,
  and you know more clearly who that self is.
Not only do you understand yourself and your life better,
  but you can see others with greater awareness, more compassion.
In fact, you can see *all* life with greater awareness,
  all existence,
    all creation.
The poet Henry Wadsworth Longfellow wrote in his later years,
  As the evening twilight fades away
  The sky is filled with stars, invisible by day.
In the fading light there is so much for you to see,
  ever so much.

Wisdom is with the aged,
and understanding in length of days.

JOB 12:12

If the doors of perception were cleansed,
everything would appear as it is, infinite.

WILLIAM BLAKE

In my fortieth year, I was as clear and decided on some subjects
as at present, and, in many respects, superior to my present self;
yet, now, in my eightieth, I possess advantages
which I would not exchange for these.

JOHANN VON GOETHE

- Travel back in time to when you were twenty or thirty. If possible, read old letters or journals you wrote at that time. What were your hopes and ambitions—things you thought were important—at that age? Then think about the things and people that worried or disturbed you then. Do any of those memories bring a smile? How would you describe your hopes, irritations, and worries today? What accounts for the differences? Are you pleased with the changes?

- Imagine that you can stand on a high mountain and look down at the events of your life. (Imagine you're writing a novel about it.) What patterns and themes can you see? How would you describe the ebb and flow of your life? If you had to describe your life's story in just one sentence, what would it be? How would you conclude your life's story? Try writing out your thoughts.

- Take a slow walk in nature, noticing whatever attracts your eye. When you're back at home, reflect on the way in which you viewed God's world and how you responded to it. Then ask yourself how you might have done that walk much earlier in your life: what you might have seen and not seen, what you might have felt and not felt. Bring a reminder of your walk—a stone, a twig, a shell—indoors and place it somewhere where your eyes can rest on it from time to time.

Remembering your past is the way to your future.

A popular adage goes, "Leave your past behind."
A popular tendency is to put the past out of your mind
   so you can move ahead with your future.
There is another way.
And that way is to remember:
   to remember people who helped you become the person you are;
   to remember events in your life that proved to be turning points,
     when your life went *this* way
       rather than that;
   to remember the adversities you lived through,
     and how you lived through them,
       and what strengths you gained, what lessons you learned;
   to remember the fond moments in your life
     when the world seemed to stand still for an instant,
       and love seemed to go on forever.

There is value in remembering your past: by reliving it in your mind
     you don't attempt to repeat it in your life.
Nor do you try to forget it.
You *can't* forget it, because it is an integral part of who you are.
This is not a matter of dwelling on the past.
It's a matter of giving the past its due,
     so the present can be richer,
          so the future can hold a brighter dawn.
Remembering your past means remembering your spiritual past:
     the stories that first gave you faith, and later restored your hope;
          those forebears who first gave you wisdom, and later, courage;
               those practices that gave meaning to your days.
Because all of them can help you find faith and hope,
     wisdom and courage, yet today.
All you have to do is remember,
     and your memory will lead you into the future.

I consider the days of old,
I remember the years long ago.
I commune with my heart in the night;
I meditate and I search my spirit.

PSALM 77:5–6

Respect the past in the full measure of its deserts,
but do not make the mistake of confusing it with the present,
nor seek in it the ideals of the future.

JOSÉ INGENIEROS

We must always have old memories
and young hopes.

ARSENE HOUSSAYE

- Develop a chronology of your life. Record important events in the order they occurred. Date them either by the year or by your age at the time. Use a highlighter to color milestones or turning points. You might want to do this in several sittings because you'll probably remember more things as time goes by. Preserve this record for yourself and for future generations.

- Create a scrapbook autobiography. Include pictures of yourself and those you love. Add anything you wish: places you lived, jobs, vacations, friends, special projects you participated in. Don't forget births and deaths, marriages and graduations, pets and autos. Write down what you want to remember about each addition—on the book pages or backs of pictures, the margins of news-paper clippings, announcements, maps, souvenirs, etc. Someday the book will make a wonderful gift for special relatives or loved ones.

- Recall two people who had the most positive influence on your life, on the person you have become. Think all the way back to your early years. In your mind, describe each of those people in detail. Explore what attracted you to them. Then write them a letter telling how you are doing and why you are thinking of them. Thank them for what they've meant to you.

- Trace your family tree. Go back as far as possible. Talk to family members, check old records, see what you can find in a genealogy library. Make several copies and share them with other members of your family.

As you learn to let go, you will gain.

There is a time in life for letting go,
    for surrendering to forces you cannot control
        and even to forces you can.
This may be a difficult task for you, one you're not used to.
By practicing the art of letting go,
    you come to the place where your life has always been leading you.
In the past so much of your energy has been spent
    on growing, on gaining, on keeping.
So much of your life has been invested in doing,
    so that you *were* what you *did*.
There is another way.
You can have value, not for what you perform,
    but for who you are.
Not in your doing,
    but in your being.

You can let go of experiences that have limited you, and be open.

You can let go of hurts that have bound you, and be forgiving.

You can let go of your natural inclination to make life go "your way"
and allow life to go the way you are led.

You can refrain from grasping, and be open to receiving.

You can accept all that you have for what it is: a gift—
a gift from that benevolent Source that is behind all that is
and all that shall ever be.

Three hundred years ago a woman named Glückel of Hameln
spoke the truth that everyone must learn:

No matter what you may lose, be patient.

For nothing belongs. It is only lent.

As you learn to let go, you allow all that is lent to return to its Source.

That includes you and your life, too.

And in that return, nothing is lost
and everything is gained.

Our letting go is in order that God might be God in us.

MEISTER ECKHART

Lord, you gave me health and I forgot you.
You take it away and I come back to you.
What infinite compassion that God, in order to give himself to me,
takes away his gifts which I allowed to come between me and him.
Lord, take away everything that is not you.
All is yours. You are the Lord.
Dispose everything, comforts, success, health.
Take all the things that possess me instead of you
that I may be wholly yours.

FRANÇOIS FÉNELON

- Make a list of things you have let go of through the years—possessions, friends, habits, emotions, physical traits, ambitions, etc. Then ask yourself: What does this list say about my life? About the nature of life itself? About my resilience? About my growth? Perhaps another person you know can make a similar list. Compare notes. Talk about what you both have learned and gained through your acts of letting go.

- Make a list of things you still need to let go of: habits that enslave you, grudges and painful memories you've carried far too long. Write a prayer for each item on your list, asking for strength to let go. Rip up the list and throw it away. Keep the prayers to use in your daily meditations.

- Go through a closet, a desk, a trunk. Pull out things you've been saving and sort them into piles. Which do you really want or need to keep? Which could be donated to a charity? Which could be pitched? Look at what is left with a careful eye. Which items would make wonderful keepsakes for family or friends—gifts rich in memories and family heritage? (Pieces of childhood clothes made into an heirloom quilt, a scrapbook of letters and souvenirs, a family cookbook filled with favorite recipes, etc.) Then begin work on one or two special gifts. As you "let go" of each treasure, you'll pass along a priceless piece of yourself to those you love.

To find the sacred place, stop right where you are.

Part of your spiritual journey is a search for the sacred.

People often travel great distances to find it.

They look for grandeur, for majesty, for vastness.

But by this season of your life,
    the truth becomes more obvious.

Every bud, every blossom, every flower
    points not to itself but beyond itself.

Every plant, every bush, every tree is a sign, and more than a sign.

Every color is a reminder that beauty is with you each step of the way,
    and it was placed there for you to find.

Every leaf and every blade is a reflection of the Divine hand.

Every simplicity is nothing less than part of the Designer's grand scheme.

Twenty centuries ago the Greek writer Epictetus,
approaching the end of his own life,
said it best as a prayer:

I thank Thee a thousand times over
that Thou hast chosen to admit me there
where I can see Thy works manifested,
and see before my eyes
the order with which Thou dost govern this universe.

All that need be added is *Amen*.

"*Surely the Lord is in this place; and I did not know it...
How awesome is this place! This is none other than the house of God;
and this is the gate of heaven.*"

GENESIS 28:16–17

*I want creation to penetrate you with so much admiration
that everywhere, wherever you may be, the least place
may bring to you the clear remembrance of the Creator.*

SAINT BASIL

All the way to heaven is heaven.

CATHERINE OF SIENA

*There are only two ways to live your life.
One is as though nothing is a miracle.
The other is as though everything is a miracle.*

ALBERT EINSTEIN

- If possible, find an isolated spot outside in nature. Sit and be quiet for an extended period. Look around you slowly, with appreciative eyes. Listen carefully to every sound. Soak up all the smells. Say a prayer of thanksgiving with your eyes wide open. Consider reading Psalm 19:1–6, one sentence at a time, while you're sitting there. Allow the psalmist's words to direct your attention to whatever is around you.

- Plant a bulb indoors. Nurture it and watch it grow. Look at it closely every day, watching the beauty and new life emerge before your eyes.

- Create a small area near your favorite chair or your bed that contains reminders of the sacred. You could include one or more symbols of your faith, a candle you can light from time to time, a Bible or prayer book, a piece of religious art, a vase that you keep filled with flowers. You might use this spot to meditate and reflect, or simply to remind you of God's abiding presence.

- Go to a favorite spiritual site—a sanctuary, for instance—at a time when you can be alone. Soak up the silence, the symbols, the smells, the memories. Pray your own prayer or allow the words of a favorite traditional prayer to guide you.

Your time of endings is best marked by new beginnings.

As life begins its retreat,
    it may appear that the ending time
        is a time only of endings.
Nothing is further from the truth.
Life does not come to a halt in autumn;
    it readies itself for what comes next.
Life does not slowly disappear;
    it busies itself for an unfolding reappearance.
At its truest and its best,
    autumn is a time of transformation.
Freed from what you had to do and who you had to be,
    you can proceed to do what you're meant to do,
        and, especially, to be who you're meant to be.

You can let die in you what needs to die, what deserves to die.

And you can bring to light those parts of you that are eager to be born:

new ways of seeing yourself,

new ways of exploring who you are as a creature of God,

new ways of relating to other people
who are also creatures of God,

new ways of connecting with everything on earth
and beyond earth.

The poet Emily Dickinson put it this way:

We turn not older with years,
but newer every day.

New life is more than a possibility.

It is a promise.

Let us not grow so as to become old after being new,
but let the newness itself grow.

SAINT AUGUSTINE

In old age they still produce fruit;
they are always green and full of sap,
showing that the Lord is upright;
he is my rock, and there is no unrighteousness in him.

PSALM 92:14–15

To be old is a glorious thing when one has not unlearned
what it means "to begin."

MARTIN BUBER

- Think back over times in your life that were new beginnings. What did they have in common? (Think about your feelings, your apprehensions, the effort required, the shifts in perspective, the results and effects on your life.) Select the one time that carries strongest memories. Write about that event and especially about all the feelings you had.

- Make a list of things you would like to try—things you've never done before, or things you haven't done in a long, long time. From this list select one thing that you will attempt. Ask someone to help you get started if this will help. Keep your list for two purposes: to add to it as your ideas grow, and to select each next new thing to try.

- Resolve to do something new every day. Read a different author, or listen to a kind of music you don't normally tune in to. Read the sections of your newspaper in a different order. Take a walk through a new neighborhood. Spend time with someone you don't normally see. Eat something you've never tried before.

- Spend time with a child or among children. Invite someone over to visit, or go to a playground, or volunteer to watch a friend's child for a short period of time. Listen. Watch. Learn. Observe how they think, how they see the world. Listen to the kinds of questions they ask. Work on a project with a child: paint a picture, cook or bake something, model with clay, or build something. Be open to what this creature of God can teach you.

There is only one time to live in, and that time is now.

From your experience with life, you know how tempting it is
to try to live in the future—
especially when you think there is so much future to live in.
You know how easy it is to be distracted from the present moment—
especially when those distractions are labeled "important."
Then you come to a time when you understand
what poets and mystics and artists have been saying all along:
there is no moment but the present moment,
there is no time but now.
It is not the length of your days that matters;
it is the width and breadth of them.
It is not how many hours and days you are given;
it is how many moments you fill
and how well you fill them.

The secret of truly living is to truly live:
to truly feel what you feel,
to truly see all that your eyes can see,
to truly savor all that is yours to savor.
An old Russian proverb says,

Every day is a messenger of God.

And so it is.

Every day announces, "You have been given a gift. Enjoy it."

Every day proclaims, "All you need is here. Use it."

Every day declares, "This is the day the Lord has made. Rejoice in it."

A thirteenth-century Persian poet named Rumi wrote:

Each moment contains a hundred messages from God.

To each cry of "O Lord," God answers, "I am here."

Remember that a hundred messages are being sent to you right now,
moment by moment.

And remember that each message says, "I am here."

One ought, every day at least, to hear a little song,
read a good poem, see a fine picture, and, if it were possible,
to speak a few reasonable words.

JOHANN VON GOETHE

Do not worry about tomorrow.

MATTHEW 6:34

Who can tell what a day may bring forth?
· Cause us, therefore, precious God,
to live every day as if it were our last,
for we know not but it may be such.

THOMAS Á KEMPIS

- Every so often in the course of this day, stop whatever you are doing and ask yourself, "Is there anything of potential enjoyment around me right now that I am missing?" If there is, enjoy it! At the end of the day, call a friend and share what you discovered.

- Try making a "time study" of a day in your life. On the night before you begin, divide a sheet of paper into one-hour increments: 7:00–8:00, 8:00–9:00, etc. (It will work best if you keep your record in a notebook you can carry with you throughout the day.) The following morning, begin to keep track of how you spend each hour. At the end of the day, look over your "time study." Evaluate your day according to how much you enjoyed the time, how fully you lived each hour, and how many hours might have been spent in more fulfilling, renewing activities.

- Choose one of your senses to honor with special attention for an entire day. If you select "taste," for instance, be especially sensitive to all tastes you experience throughout the day. Enjoy favorite foods and try new ones. Eat and drink slowly and appreciatively. Notice the variations in flavor and texture. Whatever you taste, really be aware of it. The next day, select another sense to explore.

- If you are not familiar with relaxation techniques, learn one or two. Read a book about relaxation, rent a videotape on relaxation techniques, or ask someone who is knowledgeable. Then at least once a day practice relaxation for at least twenty minutes. Not only will you feel more refreshed, you'll enjoy your days more.

In your smallness you will find your greatness.

Early in your life, you believed that what happened to you
was all that mattered.
Later, you came to feel that what happened to you
was, if not all that mattered, at least very important.
And now there comes the time in life when you realize,
however much you've done,
how little you've done;
however much your significance,
how insignificant you are.
And in recognizing your smallness, you achieve your greatness.
Because when you come to realize
that you are only a child,
you also come to know
that you are a child of God.

You have been singled out and named.

You have been given your own place and your own time on earth.

You have been formed as one part of the grand plan for all creation.

You are unlike anyone else who has ever lived.

In his autumn years, the English poet William Wordsworth
shared what he had learned:

> *Trailing clouds of glory do we come*
> *From God, who is our home.*

You have come trailing clouds of glory—
a glory that comes not from who you are,
but from Whose you are;
a glory that comes not from what you've accomplished,
but from what is being accomplished in you.

You have come trailing clouds of glory from God.

Even you.

Especially you.

*From within or from behind a light shines through us upon things
and makes us aware that we are nothing, but the light is all.*

RALPH WALDO EMERSON

*It is difficult to make a man feel miserable
when he feels he is worthy of himself
and claims kindred to the great God who made him.*

ABRAHAM LINCOLN

*Govern all by your wisdom, O Lord,
so that my soul may always be serving you as you will,
and not as I may choose. Let me die to myself,
that so I may serve you: let me live for you,
who in yourself are the true life.*

TERESA OF AVILA

- As you grow older and your perspective about your importance and your ambitions changes, take a look around to discover what you can offer to others. What needs do you see in your family, friends, community? Who are some people you could help—in small, thoughtful ways? From this new perspective, jot down ideas for using your unique gifts to make a difference in the lives of those around you. Idea starters: volunteer in a nursing home, serve in a food shelter, telephone or visit persons who are confined to their homes or lonely, write letters to distant relatives, start reading or discussion groups, talk with friends who are apprehensive about growing older. Discover true greatness through these new and unique uses of your gifts.

- Write your own affirmation of faith. In one paragraph try to capture exactly what you have come to believe about God, how God already has been active in and through your life, how God will be revealed and expressed in the years ahead. Read this creed to yourself each night before retiring. Use it as a daily basis for meditation and prayer, and add to it with each new discovery.

- If you haven't done so already, give some thought to how you would like your specialness to be honored at the end of your life on earth. If you have ideas about how you'd like to spend your final days, about important keepsakes, about a certain legacy you'd like to pass along, or about the way you'd like to be remembered, now is a good time to communicate your wishes, either on paper or in conversation with loved ones.

There is no way but this: the way of love.

Follow your path long enough and it will converge with other paths.
Live your life deeply enough and it will merge with other lives,
   and with all of life.
Go in search of that which gives your life meaning
   and you will return with one word on your lips.
That word, in its many forms, is *love*.
It is possible to be too young to love,
   but you can never be too old.
In many ways, the older you are, the better you can love.
The more experiences you have lived through,
   the better you can understand the experiences of those around you.
The more you have cherished others and been cherished by others,
   the more naturally your life will overflow with affection.
The more you have witnessed and felt the boundless love of God,
   the more that love can be expressed through you.

You're never too old to love.

And you're never too old to begin loving.

No matter what has happened to you before,
   you can love today.

No matter what you have missed and what you have regretted,
   you can love today.

No matter what has been taken from you or what you surrendered,
   you can love today.

And because of who you are and what you have experienced,
   you can love in a way that someone less experienced cannot.

When the seasons of your life draw to a close,
   what will matter most is not how much you have known.

What will matter most is how much you have loved.

*Love is the only thing we can carry with us where we go,
and it makes the end so easy.*

LOUISA MAY ALCOTT

*If I speak in the tongues of mortals and of angels,
but do not have love, I am a noisy gong or a clanging cymbal.
And if I have prophetic powers, and understand all mysteries
and all knowledge, and if I have all faith, so as to remove
mountains, but do not have love, I am nothing.*

1 CORINTHIANS 13:1–2

*Love every leaf, every ray of God's light. Love the plants,
love the animals, love everything. If you love everything,
you will sense the divine mystery in things. Once you sense it,
you will begin to understand it better every day.
And you will come at last to love the whole world.*

FYODOR DOSTOEVSKY

- Form a clear mental image of the person who has been most loving in your life. What did they do that made them that way? Pretend they could inhabit your body for a time. What might they be doing now—right where you are, among the people you know? Once you have determined that, try it out yourself—for their sake if for no one else's. If you enjoy the experience, try something similar on another day. Who knows where this could lead?

- List the people you especially love. Pray for them daily. Select one person at a time from your list and keep them especially close in your thoughts for a day or two. Write them a note or a letter to let them know you're thinking about them. Tell them why you love them so and what you admire in them.

- Now try the same experiment with people you find especially hard to love. Pray for them daily. Ask for guidance in discovering things to love and admire in these people—and make a true effort to see those things. Then select one person at a time from this list and keep them close in your thoughts for a day or two. Try writing them a note to let them know you're thinking about them, and tell them what you appreciate in them.

- Give someone a symbol of your love for no reason other than you want to. Your gift need not have monetary value; in fact, some of the most meaningful gifts have no monetary value whatsoever. Give them something you have created, or something that has been a part of your life for a long time, or something that reminds them of your affection.

The English poet Alfred, Lord Tennyson, wrote about life's final years:

Though much is taken, much abides.

His words are true.

Come the autumn of your life, much has been taken.

Much cannot be recaptured.

But much abides.

In fact, of what is really important in your life, *more* abides.

By the autumn of your life, you've done so much,
   and been so many places.
You've seen so much,
   and learned so many things about life.
Yet you also know that even more adventures lie ahead.
There are still moments in time for you to fill,
   and so many ways to fill them.
There are still sacred places for you to visit,
   and they're all around you.
There is still love for you to share,
   and people to share it with.
There is still meaning for you to find,
   and every reason to find it.
There are still new paths for you to explore,
   and a faithful Guide to lead you.

A prayer composed thousands of years ago by the writer of Psalm 90
is as appropriate today as ever:

Teach us to number our days,

that we may get a heart of wisdom.

May you learn to number each of your days

by the way you live

and by the way you love.

May you learn to make every one of your days count

by the way you remember

and by the way you look forward.

May you come to that time when you receive

that which gives your life both meaning and purpose:

a heart of wisdom.

AUTUMN WISDOM
Finding Meaning in Life's Later Years

Cover and interior design by Melanie Lawson

Scripture quotations are from the New Revised Standard Version Bible, copyright © 1989 by the Division of Christian Education of the National Council of the Churches of Christ in the U.S.A. and used by permission, and from the Revised Standard Version of the Bible, copyright © 1946, 1952, 1971 by the Division of Christian Education of the National Council of the Churches of Christ in the U.S.A. and used by permission.

Library of Congress Cataloging-in-Publication Data

Miller, James E., 1945–
    Autumn wisdom: finding meaning in life's later years / James E. Miller.
        p. cm.
    Includes bibliographical references
    ISBN 0-8066-2834-0 (alk. paper)
    1. Middle aged persons—Religious life. 2. Aged—Religious life. 3. Christian life—Methodist authors.
4. Meditations. 5. Middle aged persons—Psychology. 6. Aged—Psychology. I. Title.
BV4579.5.M54   1995
242'.65—dc20   95-21562
                                                                                CIP